Mindpower
secrets

The experts tell all!

About the author

Martin Manser BA (Hons), MPhil teaches communication skills at the London College of Communication. He is a language trainer and consultant, and also a reference book editor. Among his books are *Time Management* and *Presenting,* also in the **business secrets** series.

Author's note

The author would like to thank Hannah Murphy, Hannah Harris, Sara James and Roger Manser for their help and advice.

Mindpower
secrets

Collins

A division of HarperCollins*Publishers*

77-85 Fulham Palace Road, London W6 8JB

www.BusinessSecrets.net

First published in Great Britain in 2010 by HarperCollins*Publishers*
Published in Canada by HarperCollins*Canada*. www.harpercollins.ca
Published in Australia by HarperCollins*Australia*. www.harpercollins.com.au
Published in India by HarperCollins*PublishersIndia*. www.harpercollins.co.in

2

A catalogue record for this book is available from the British Library.

ISBN 978-0-00-734676-9

Printed and bound at Clays Ltd, St Ives plc

Contents

Unlock the potential of your mind

The mind in each one of us has the incredible capacity for thinking, understanding and decision making. This book explores how you can release the potential that is already within you.

In my working life, I've had to make many strategic decisions about which direction to take. Some decisions have been easy; others have come about only through much concentrated effort and creative problem solving. Some of the ways in which my work has developed have also arisen out of discoveries that have been made, it seems, by 'chance': being in the right time and the right place and having the right experience. Further, in the many presentations that I have given, I have had to expand my memory to remember, not only broad facts and important details, but also people's names. So, in a way, I wish that I had had this book in my hands years ago – it would have helped me greatly!

I wish you all the best as you personally undertake one of life's greatest journeys, to explore and use the resources of your mind.

This book consists of 50 **secrets**, set out in seven chapters:

■ **Understand how your mind works.** Knowing what kind of person you are is an important first step to challenging yourself and developing the full use of your mind.

■ **Read and listen more effectively.** Improving your skills in the key perceptive areas of reading and listening will help you keep ahead of your competitors.

■ **Think strategically.** It's all too easy for your thinking to go round and round in circles and not make progress, so here are some practical tips to kick-start your thinking processes.

■ **Solve problems well.** Here we apply various mindpower techniques to help you develop a wider range of ways for dealing with difficulties and making decisions.

■ **Develop your memory.** Here is useful guidance to help you deal with the difficulties we all have in remembering information, names and numbers.

■ **Focus your mind.** To work effectively in today's business environment, you need to be focused, giving the tasks in hand your full attention and cultivating a positive outlook and attitude towards any problems that you face.

■ **Inspire your mind.** You need to stimulate and nurture your mind to be able to manage – and if possible reduce – stress levels and become successful as you work with colleagues and manage your time effectively.

If you follow these seven **secrets**, you will be well on your way to making the best use of the vast resources that are already at your disposal in your mind.

This book will help you unlock the vast resources of your mind.

Understand how your mind works

First off, it is vital to know how your mind works best, so that you can decide which learning styles are best suited to you. In this chapter, we'll address this, before exploring how you can develop methods for using your mind creatively for common tasks such as taking notes and researching a subject. It is all too easy to follow established ways of thinking, so you need to be challenged to change and develop as a whole person.

1.1

Know how your brain functions

If you are aware of the contrasting activities of the two sides of your brain – broadly, creative on the right, logical on the left – you will be able to work more effectively. Further, if you are working with colleagues in a team, make sure that the members' skills complement one another.

Activities in the brain are commonly attributed to either the right side or the left, depending on their nature in the creative/logical divide. In some people, one side of the brain is more dominant than the other.

People whose **left side** is more dominant:
■ Process information in a linear sequence easily, taking different elements and arranging them logically.
■ Process words and numbers relatively easily.
■ Enjoy analysing details and making lists.

People whose **right side** is more dominant:
■ Process information as a whole more easily. First of all they see the big picture, and then look at the details.

■ Process information creatively and intuitively, using their imagination relatively easily.
■ Are aware of spatial dimensions.
■ Enjoy learning that involves doing, feeling, touching objects and drawing illustrations in colour.

We tend to have one side of the brain that is more dominant than the other, though great scientists tend to be very well-balanced in these terms. Einstein, for exampled, enjoyed activities such as sailing, art and playing the violin.

The significance of this is:
■ If you are undeveloped on one side of the brain, work at strengthening and nurturing the unused potential of the less dominant side, so that it becomes more effective. If you do this, you will find that, rather than being weakened in the area in which you are currently stronger, you will actually become stronger in both areas, and the overall performance of your mind will be improved.

■ Make sure that a team of colleagues working together has a balance of those who enjoy logical, analytical thinking and those whose style is more intuitive and creative.

Work at developing your brain's unused potential.

1.2

Strengthen the right side of your brain

If the left side of your brain is more dominant, then it's time to strengthen the right side so that you become more balanced.

There are many ways in which you could strengthen the right side of your brain. They include:

■ **Dream dreams.** Remove yourself from your cold analysis and use your imagination. You could even write down your dreams.

■ **See the big picture.** Go beyond the details in which you are immersed and see the widest possible dimensions.

> **case study** By personality, the left side of my brain is more dominant. After leading seminars on writing clear English, I realized that I needed to branch out as the market place was becoming saturated. I wrestled with this problem for some time, trying logically to think through ways of dealing with it. One day, when I was not thinking about this problem, the thought

■ **Take risks.** Don't always be cautious and play it safe (but don't be reckless!). Do something you usually do differently – go a different way to work; experiment with different foods or ways of cooking.

■ **Change your perspective.** Be on the lookout for positive ways of grasping new opportunities, rather than seeing them as a threat.

■ **Be creative.** Think of imaginative ways of expressing a problem you are currently dealing with. Draw it, or something that could represent it. What colour would it be? What shape and dimensions?

■ **Take a break from work.** Do something physically active – go to the gym, go dancing. A healthy body will develop a healthy mind.

■ **Develop your intuition.** When random thoughts occur to you when you are doing something that is unrelated to work, such as having a shower or driving home from work, don't ignore them. Give them your attention: these thoughts come from your subconscious.

Take something you usually do and do it differently.

struck me: I should intentionally target managers who had deliberately chosen a career that didn't initially involve writing. In particular, I focused on accountants and engineers. The success lay in being open to fresh, 'outside-the-box' thinking and then being proactive: actively deciding a new strategy and formulating a plan to capture a new market.

1.3

Strengthen the left side of your brain

If the right side of your brain is more dominant, then it's time to strengthen the left side to achieve that elusive but rewarding balance.

Again, there are many ways in which you could strengthen the left side of your brain. Here are a few:

■ **Delve into the details.** Go beyond the big picture to fill in details. If you're not sure what details to think about, answer the following question words: 'who?', 'where?', 'when?', 'what?', 'how?' and 'why?'

■ **Become more organized.** Make a list of things you need to do. Make notes.

one minute wonder Give yourself dates for achieving goals. Break the goals down into manageable and timed tasks so that you have clear and definite scheduled tasks. Commit yourself to doing that, and tell a friend or colleague to contact you a day after the set time to make sure you have done it.

"He that cannot reason is a fool. He that will not is a bigot. He that dare not is a slave."

Andrew Carnegie, Scottish-born industrialist and philanthropist

■ **Plan ahead.** Think of a task that you need to do. Work out all the steps that you need to take to achieve that aim. Then put all those stages in the most logical order to fulfil them most effectively.

■ **Think in the long term.** Set yourself long-term goals and then analyse those goals, working out intermediate steps that are realistic and achievable. It's important to write them down: putting them down on paper will help you visualize and concentrate on the goals.

■ **Take firm decisions.** Switch off the television earlier than usual to get more sleep. Resolve to develop new, beneficial habits, such as walking more, going to the gym or playing chess. Get friends to help you if necessary, or use local clubs.

■ **Train yourself to become more logical.** Work at solving puzzles, such as Sudoku or crossword puzzles, however easy or difficult they are.

■ **Train your memory.** Deliberately set yourself to learn phone numbers or spellings that you find difficult to remember.

Go beyond the big picture and begin to fill in the details.

1.4

Identify your learning style

People learn in different ways. If you want to use your mind effectively, you will need to know the best way in which you learn. There are three main styles of learning, which are allied to our senses.

■ **Visual learners.** Such people like to see information in pictures, diagrams, charts, tables and in writing.
■ **Auditory learners.** They like to listen to information and then discuss it, listening to what others say to help them learn.
■ **Kinesthetic learners.** These people like to be active and learn by doing. They are attuned to the feel and movement of things.

case study The original working group that met to develop a new marketing strategy was made up of three academically inclined graduates, Stephen, Andrew and Greta, who were very gifted at logical and verbal arguments. They loved to discuss the detailed wording of the strategy and tactics, but never made any real progress on the main part of the campaign.

Personal learning

Knowing where your preferences lie is the first step. You can then use that knowledge as a basis to challenge yourself to extend your range of learning styles. The aim is to be balanced and well-adjusted so that you learn in ways that are less familiar to you and are not your preferred style. Seek opportunities to practise a different style.

Team development

If you work in a team, make sure that other members of the team have different learning styles so that you complement one another.

Presentations

If you are presenting information to others, you should be aware that people learn in different ways. Good presenters use a multi-sensory approach to include different styles of learning so that every member of the audience is able to take in the presentation effectively. This means that you should provide visual aids that illustrate your argument, give headings to support it, and provide opportunities for discussion and further expression through stories and role play.

If you work in a team, make sure that its members have different learning styles to complement one another.

When Ros joined the committee, everything changed. Her skills were on the creative and visual, 'thinking outside-the-box' side. She quickly enabled the whole group to move on, as she drew pattern diagrams and flow charts of the work involved. This new way of working resulted in fresh ideas that stirred the whole committee into action to tackle the campaign.

1.5

Unleash your creativity

The American inventor Thomas Edison said, "Genius is one percent inspiration and ninety-nine percent perspiration". You develop your creativity by hard work… and also by allowing room to receive and harness inspiration, when it comes.

Here are five steps to help you develop your creative thinking.

1 **Change your way of doing things.** Read more widely; pick up a magazine on a subject that you don't normally look at or read a novel by an author unfamiliar to you. Take up a new hobby – you don't have to be the best in the world; just enjoy it. It'll help you develop your personality.

> **case study** The music market in around 2001 was in a mess: CDs were expensive and were difficult to transport; MP3 players were poor quality and short on memory; and it was difficult to get hold of MP3 files

2 **Be open to fresh ideas.** A new thought or solution to a problem may suddenly occur to you, especially when you are not thinking directly about the problem. Evaluate the insight that has come to you, and test it to see if it is useful and worth pursuing. For more on thinking creatively, see Secret 3.4.

3 **Prepare.** If you are giving a presentation, there is no substitute for working hard on research to make sure you have all the relevant facts. Perhaps you don't know where to start? A mind map may help you (see Secret 1.6).

4 **Analyse the facts.** Think them through and examine them from different angles. Challenge assumptions and distinguish between facts and opinions. Explore weaknesses and find gaps in an argument. Think through the reasons why something has developed as it has. Uncover the background causes of an event. Analyse all data critically.

5 **Put the facts together (synthesize them).** Evaluate different options. Think of new ways of putting things together. For example, you may think of developing better systems at work: a combination of logic and creativity will help you do this.

Give yourself space to be imaginative and come up with exciting new ideas.

legally and easily. The creative combination of Apple's iPod and iTunes solved all these problems and also gave the company 75% dominance of the digital music market in both hardware and software.

1.6

Draw a pattern diagram

A pattern diagram is a creative drawing that captures what you judge to be the main aspects of a central thought that you want to consider.

Many people find drawing a pattern diagram (also called a mind map, pattern notes or a spider diagram) helpful to see all the parts of a subject and how they fit together. It can be useful for taking notes, brainstorming a topic or researching a subject. Here's how to prepare a pattern diagram in seven steps:

1 Take a blank sheet of A4 paper and place it on the table in a landscape format.

2 Write with a pencil your central subject (a word or a few words, not a whole sentence) in the middle of the paper.

case study In order to plan a course on Report Writing, I used a pattern diagram to write down all I knew about the audience: their needs, what they already knew and the level of proficiency I wanted

3 Write around that central word other key words that relate to it; let your imagination move you. Think of subdivisions of that subject, or facts that relate to the subject.

4 Keep branching out various other aspects of the subject that come into your mind. These other aspects can cover a variety of points, such as facts relating to the subject, your feelings about a subject, and the advantages or disadvantages of following different courses of action. If you get stuck at any point, stimulate your thinking by answering the question words: 'who?', 'where?', 'when?', 'what?', 'how?' and 'why?'

5 At this stage, do not reject any thoughts. (Use an eraser only sparingly to delete what you have written.)

6 You could colour in different key words to show which ones are related. You could also use symbols, images or pictures if you find that helpful.

7 You could also number the different key words to give them a hierarchy of importance.

Let your imagination stimulate you, and you will be able to draw a pattern diagram that captures the different aspects of a subject.

them to achieve. I broke down the major points that I wanted them to learn into manageable chunks. During the seminar, it really helped to have a clear summary that I could refer to on one sheet of paper.

1.7

Change your thinking

It's all too easy to think in the same way that we are used to – for our thoughts, feelings and habits to get stuck in a rut. This need not last, however: you can learn to think differently!

Ways to help you think differently:

■ **Try a new approach.** Move on from the "we've-always-done-it-this-way" approach and rethink things, both logically and creatively.
■ **Think positively.** If you tend to always raise objections about how and why something won't work, stop yourself and try to view a situation constructively instead. If you combine your natural caution with a new optimism, you may be able to improve the plans.
■ **Reconsider yourself and your career.** Look at your work situation from a fresh perspective. Is there room for improvement?

case study The British designer and engineer James Dyson challenged accepted ways of thinking when, in the 1980s, he launched the first bagless vacuum cleaner. He had been frustrated by the way that conventional cleaners lose power as the bags fill up with dust and dirt. Delivering more power to the

■ **Think creatively.** Change from narrow to original thinking. If you have trouble developing innovative, creative ideas, try using a device such as the pattern diagram (Secret 1.6) to help fire your imagination.

■ **Change your habits.** It can help to learn new skills in order to give you a broader set of tools for tackling work and solving problems.

All of these ways of thinking differently involve taking risks. If you are naturally cautious, you may be unwilling to take risks. Think why this is. Here are some possible reasons:

■ "I don't want to make a fool of myself." The response to this is simply, "does this really matter?"

■ "It might not work out." The response to this is to quote the saying, "a person who never made mistakes never made anything".

■ "It'll take a long time." Well yes, it may, but think how you learnt to drive or how you learnt a foreign language. Weren't these incredibly worthwhile skills that took some time to learn?

Just because you have done things in a certain way in the past doesn't mean you have to follow that way always. You can change your way of working.

vacuum cleaner may have been one (partial) solution, but instead, Dyson adopted a different way of thinking. He started from the premise that vacuum cleaners were no longer 'allowed' to have bags, and this led him to devise an entirely different approach – the cyclone system – which has proved remarkably successful.

1.8

Develop as a whole person

We are not just people who think. We are humans – sentient, emotional, physical beings. And as part of developing mind power, you need to develop yourself as a whole human being.

Here is a list to prompt and encourage your development.

■ **Break your normal routine.** You can start in an easy fashion simply by watching different programmes on television; seek out a more diverse range of programmes than you usually watch.

■ **Read about current affairs.** Devour your favourite website, a quality newspaper or periodical such as *The Economist* or *Newsweek*.

■ **Think. Don't just read.** Think about the big underlying issues to problems, news stories and other narratives. Take time to reflect. Schedule in time to relax your mind from concentrated action.

■ **Challenge yourself.** Move out of your comfort zone. For example, I recently was a student for a four-week intensive course – I found the experience demanding as it was 35 years since I was last a student on an educational course!

■ **Jot and sketch.** Carry a pencil and notebook, or electronic equivalent, with you to jot down or sketch fresh ideas as they come to you.

one minute wonder Rather than working through your lunch break, go out and look around you. Break your routine: buy sandwiches from a different shop, go to a different café or order different food. Look around you with a fresh pair of eyes, take in the sights, smells and sounds. Imagine you've just landed in your city as a tourist – what would you notice?

■ **Learn to listen.** But don't just listen … really listen. What are people saying and not saying? Reflect on what you're learning. Talk with friends and colleagues. Discuss issues and ideas; express your latest thinking to gauge responses.

■ **Be alert to your different senses.** Make yourself look up at the sky. Stop for a moment or two and listen to the sounds around you. Reflect on them. They are part of who you are. (Drinking Coca Cola reminds me of a family holiday in France, for example.)

■ **Absorb some culture.** Go to an art gallery or museum. Or, if that doesn't take your fancy, go to a trade exhibition.

■ **Care for others.** Don't become so absorbed with yourself that you neglect people around you, in your community and in the wider world. Engage in some practical action to be helpful.

■ **Get physical.** Take up a physical sport such as jogging, cycling or swimming. As well as the health benefits, it will help relax your mind.

■ **Express your artistic side.** If you are creatively inclined, fit that into your regular schedule.

■ **Meditate.** Spend time in a form of prayer or meditation to help you connect with more than the physical world.

We are whole people and need to develop different aspects of our lives.

Read and listen more effectively

Knowing your aims in reading and being able to read texts quickly are important skills. Taking in, thinking about and understanding what you read is also vital so that you can keep ahead of the game. We read not only words but also numbers in charts, graphs and diagrams, and there are techniques you can learn to improve how to read these. Listening, evaluating and then asking appropriate questions are also key skills that you need to cultivate.

2.1

Know your aims in reading

When reading a document, it is important to know the reasons why you are reading it. Are you reading to gain specific knowledge of certain details? Or are you reading to gain an overall grasp of a subject? Knowing your purpose will determine the approach you choose to follow.

Different reasons for reading include:

1 To get an overall idea of the text – this is known as skim-reading or gist-reading.

2 To gain a lot of detailed understanding of information in the text – this is known as intensive reading

case study Depak was given the brief to research the background of moving into a new market for mobile phones. He quickly found the best websites and

> **"A capacity and taste for reading gives access to whatever has already been discovered by others"**
>
> **Abraham Lincoln, US President 1861–1865**

3 To find a specific piece of information – this is known as scan reading.

4 To understand the writer's purpose in the text. Because the writer's purpose may be implicit rather than explicit, this is known as reading to infer.

We use different reading techniques at different times. For example, to look at a job advertisement to see if we might apply for the job, we will gist-read to gain a general understanding of whether we want to take things further. In looking at a website for a phone number of a company, we will scan-read the company's homepage to locate the 'Contact us' page and then find the phone number. If we have to conduct research in writing a background paper on a new product, then we will have to undertake intensive reading of texts and articles to gain a lot of detailed information.

Know your purpose in reading; that will determine the approach you follow.

navigated to the appropriate pages, where he found summaries of the new market and was able to take notes and present them to his meeting.

2.2

Read more quickly

Build on the steps as outlined in the previous Secret by adding the element of speed. Having prepared to read by working out your aims, you are now ready to read through a text more quickly.

Here are some ways to help you read through a text more quickly. If you practise the techniques, your reading will speed up.

■ **Devour the text.** Rather than reading in a strictly linear way, a single word at a time, aim to read groups of words.

■ **Put a clock on it.** Set yourself a task of reading a text in a specified amount of time. If necessary, deliberately put yourself under slight pressure to read in a concentrated manner. This will mean that you should aim to reduce not only the time you spend reading each group of words but also the time you spend going back and rereading previous sections.

■ **Look for content words.** Much of a text will be taken up with function words, such as 'of', 'the', 'much', 'a', 'will', 'be' (as in this sentence). Train yourself to look for the significant words or groups of significant words in a paragraph. These will probably be the strong nouns, adjectives or verbs.

one minute wonder Take a long and difficult text that you are not looking forward to reading. Discipline yourself on this occasion to read only the first line of each paragraph. When you have finished, pause and think about what you have read. Note any questions that your reading has raised.

■ **Aim for the top.** Look especially at the first sentence at the top of each paragraph. If the text is well-written, the material contained in all the other sentences in the paragraph should in some way relate to the idea expressed in the paragraph's first sentence, expanding on it, discussing it, illustrating it, commenting on it or arguing with it. A further significance of this structure is that, if you want to compile a summary of a text, you should be able to take the first sentence of each paragraph as a basis.

■ **Look at the road signs.** Read any summary or conclusions that are provided, and use the signposts of chapter headings and subheadings for information on content and context.

■ **Keep a track of direction.** Look out for signposts such as 'furthermore' or 'in addition', which are used to reinforce a point already made. And look out for 'although' or 'alternatively', which are used to introduce a difference or contrast. Words such as 'consequently' and 'therefore' indicate a result.

Read a text in groups of words; focus on the key content words.

2.3

Take in key information

One of your aims in reading will be to absorb the information in a text in order to relate it to other people. Here again, there are pointers to help you better absorb the text you are reading.

■ **Preparation.** Before you begin, note down questions that occur to you and that you want answered about the subject. Read the text looking specifically for the answers to these questions.

■ **Read critically.** As you read, evaluate both the key messages and the detail. Note the parts with which you disagree or strongly agree, and think specifically about them. (I did this once and found myself initially disagreeing with the author, but, after some thought, I revised my initial conclusions and was persuaded by the writer's argument.)

> **case study** A few years ago Rob had to give an important presentation to his colleagues in the Human Resources Department. He was rather daunted by the prospect but, as he read through all the background papers on changes in employment law, he began to

■ **Paraphrase the main point.** Put in your own words the writer's fundamental argument. The more you can express the writer's ideas in your own words, the better. As you engage in this process, you are absorbing the text. Omit details. Summarize specific examples in more general terms. Use headings.

■ **Use your mind's creativity.** Draw a pattern diagram of the main points of the text (see Secret 1.6).

■ **Underline or highlight.** Use a pen to underline or highlight key phrases in your own copy of a book (not a copy that belongs to the library!) or a photocopy or printout of a web page.

■ **Explain the text to someone else.** Do this in person, not by email, and ask your colleague or friend to be ruthless in continually questioning, 'what do you mean?' The task is done only when they are absolutely clear about what you are trying to communicate. Be succinct, and the simpler you can express something, the better.

■ **Review your understanding.** When you have finished reading a section, pause to review it. Can you identify and recall the key points?

Having to explain a text simply to someone else is one of the most powerful ways of taking in information.

take notes, summarizing the different reasons and emphases. Gradually he came to discern his own viewpoint. Having to work through others' material not only made him aware of their views but also helped refine his own thinking and standpoint.

2.4

Learn the SQ3R reading technique

A common technique used to help you absorb written information is SQ3R: Survey, Question, Read, Recite, Review. This takes in the techniques discussed in earlier Secrets in this chapter on reading.

The **SQ3R** technique consists of the following steps:

■ **Survey** Before you start to read, survey the text. Look at chapter titles, headings and subheadings. Consult any summaries at the beginnings or ends of chapters. Read the beginnings and ends of paragraphs to try to understand the main points and gain an overview of the text.

■ **Question** Raise questions while you are reading. What is this text trying to say? What does the title mean? Turn headings into questions.

case study Andrea was not a natural reader but found the SQ3R method very helpful, especially the reciting and reviewing parts. She wrote notes, spoke them out

■ Read Obviously you now need to read the text, but do this in a concentrated way. Begin to answer some of the questions you have asked. Don't try to read too much at a time. Stop at logical points to make sure you have understood what you have just read.

■ Recite After your intensive reading, go back over the text in your mind to see how many of the main points you can recall. As you do this, you will probably notice that your memory is weak in places and you will need to read some of the material again. You could say out loud or write down the key points of what you have read. When taking notes of what you have read, you will find it very helpful to summarize the text in your own words. Adapt your reading style to your learning style (see Secret 1.4): the more senses you involve in this (e.g. hearing and speaking, not just reading), the more likely you are to remember what you have read. Use your voice to tell yourself what you've read.

■ Review Now take a break, then go back over the text quickly in an overall way to review where you've got to. If you took notes, look over these (or even cover these up and see if you can recall the most important points). Go back over any parts you need to refresh your memory.

Go back over a text you have just read to see if you can remember all the key points.

and tried explaining what she had read to her younger brother. She also reviewed what she had read after one day, three days and a week to improve her recall.

2.5

Make sense of numbers

Understanding words may come relatively easily to you, but understanding numbers may be more difficult when you are faced with bewildering lists in charts or graphs. How do you make sense of them?

Here are some simple tips to help you understand numbers and identify trends:

■ **Identify the content and remit of your data.** Take your time to work your way into the data presented to you, so that you are familiar with what it's about. What kind of a chart or graph is it? What information is it trying to convey?

■ **Read the headings and captions.** Make sure you understand what they refer to (e.g. 'budget', 'actual', 'targeted').

> **case study** Ed and his colleagues were listening to a market-research presentation for a new product that was targeted at women in the whole of North America. It was only as he closely questioned Marcus,

"It is the mark of a truly intelligent person to be moved by statistics" George Bernard Shaw, English playwright

■ **Check the units.** Do you understand the units referred to (for example, percentages or millions of people)?

■ **Check the source.** Look at who compiled the data, and when. How up to date is it?

■ **Does the format make sense?** Choose one figure and think about whether it makes sense to you in the context of any heading that has been applied to it.

■ **Differentiate separate information.** Graphs and charts are used to compare data, so distinguish separate lines on a graph and the separate elements in a bar chart, for example.

■ **Use your knowledge.** Particularly if you have a good understanding of the subject, look at each column and the highest and lowest figures – are these as you would expect? Do the same with each row.

Familiarize yourself with the data, the limits of its extent and its context. Does it make sense to you?

the colleague giving the presentation, that he discovered the sample figures were actually based on ten men in California. He learnt that day that checking the source of data being presented was very important.

2.6

Interpret statistics on graphs

As you look at statistics, it is important to evaluate them and set them in context. Only then are you able to decide on the significance of an apparent trend, for example, or to explain exceptions to general trends and accord them a level of importance.

Here are some more tips to help you interpret numbers; this time, with the emphasis on recognizing patterns and trends.

■ **Compare columns.** See if a trend is rising, falling or remaining constant. Are there any exceptions to a general trend? Try and discern patterns. Do the same with rows.

■ **Note averages and deviations.** Work out an average for a row or column, then look for variations from that. Analyse the reasons for significant differences from the average. However, bear in mind that comparing figures against an average can be misleading: it may not allow for seasonal variations, for example, or for quarterly payments if the graph or chart is divided into months. In such cases, what may be more helpful is comparing figures against a budgeted target.

■ **Look at the focus of the graph.** Check the scale on the left-hand side (vertical axis) and also if the right-hand axis is different. If the left-hand scale does not start at 0, be aware that those who prepared the graph may be focusing in on – and thereby exaggerating – a particular feature of the statistics.

■ **Ignore extrapolations.** If additional information is used in a graph that is based purely on an extrapolation of existing data, be cautious of giving it too much credence. It is speculative information.

■ **Analyse the data.** Are the exceptions to any general patterns temporary blips or do they indicate long-term trends? What do you know of the reasons for their occurence? What are the possibilities of their continuation? How significant are they?

■ **Make useful conclusions.** Write down your conclusions and check that they are borne out by any accompanying text that is meant to summarize the chart or graph.

Think whether exceptions to any general patterns are temporary blips or do they indicate long-term trends.

2.7

Listen more carefully

In these times of quick phone calls on our mobiles and instant text messaging and emails, our lives are often full of fast communication, backwards and forwards. We need to learn to slow down to be able to listen to one another more effectively. Listening is a key way we take information into our minds.

Here are the seven components of intelligent listening.

1 Focus on the other person; look at them if you can see them. Very often in conversations, while the other person is talking, we are thinking more about what we can say to them in response than actually listening to them fully. Good listening strengthens relationships.

2 Listen to the words other people are saying, of course, but go beyond that. Notice their tone and facial expressions; be aware of their feelings; when and how they pause; notice too what people are not saying.

3 Respect each person as unique; recognize they have a need and a right to express themselves as an individual.

4 Understand other people. I believe that we can only do this effectively if we are confident in ourselves as people rather than constantly being anxious about, for example, what people are thinking about us.

5 Respect people's privacy and don't delve more deeply into private matters than they want to disclose.

6 Listen out for cues that people want to disclose more of themselves and respond accordingly, perhaps by a short 'mmm', which expresses the wish to allow the other person to say more, or use a short questions to prompt them to continue. An acquaintance once said to me, "I've been really unhappy since my wife died." I gently responded, "When was that?" He told me that it had happened 12 years ago, and then talked for a long time about her. I was aware of his desire to talk and responded to his cue.

7 Reflect back: that is, summarize in a few words what the person has been saying. This shows that you are really listening and trying to understand them. They will soon put you right if you've misunderstood something.

True listening means that you recognize the other person's need to express their unique individuality. Good listening strengthens relationships.

2.8

Evaluate what you listen to

We don't simply listen to words. Our minds are called upon to apply our knowledge, understand what we are hearing and form an opinion about it.

If you want to evaluate what you are listening to, you must:

■ Distinguish between facts and opinions.
■ Detect any prejudice in what the speaker has said.
■ Divide the subjective from the objective.
■ Discern the speaker's attitude to the subject being talked about.
■ Draw conclusions from the speaker's argument. Think about the significance of what the speaker says: what are its implications?
■ Discern any differences between what the speaker is saying and the way in which they are expressing it.

Case study 1
As a consultant, Jo quickly realized that she needed to build good working relationships with her clients and gain their trust. She further knew that this meant she'd have to develop good listening skills.

"The ear of the leader must ring with the voices of the people"

Woodrow Wilson, US President 1913–1921

Companies were paying a lot of money to use her as a resource to help them. So she was thankful when, at the end of a meeting, one of the company's colleagues responded, "Jo, we really appreciate your interest in us. You're focused and open to what we have to say. You patiently listen to us. You're good at asking the right questions to gain insights into how our organization works. Thanks!"

Case study 2

Harry, a good listener, was on the board of directors. He worked closely with Sarah, the managing director. In one meeting, Sarah was talking about the promotion of a colleague called Joe, who worked in a different department. Harry picked up on the fact that the content of what Sarah was saying was inconsistent with the way in which she spoke. The tone and speed of her voice revealed surprise at the unexpected nature of Joe's promotion, betraying her own misgivings about the appointment.

Think about the meaning and significance of what the speaker says: what are the implications?

2.9

Question the speaker

As we listen to other people, questions often come into our minds about what they are saying … and sometimes also about what they are not saying.

You can ask questions in at least four situations:

■ When you want to find out more about something. Here, ask open questions – those that cannot be answered by a simple 'yes' or 'no'. This will give the person answering the question an opportunity to think and develop their response. "Why do you think sales decreased in the first quarter?", for example, or, "How can we increase staff retention rates?"

■ When you don't understand something and you want the speaker to make clear what they have just said: "Maz, I wonder if you could go over

case study Mark used to meet Jay at conferences every year or so. They had worked together briefly but he felt they had never really communicated. At one conference, they found themselves moving beyond the normal small talk, though, and managed to get past the point at which they'd always got stuck before.

> **"The important thing is not to stop questioning. Curiosity has its own reason for existing."** **Albert Einstein**

those figures again, please?", "Jack, what do you mean by …?", "Are you saying that you can supply these products by the end of the month?"

■ When you do understand what the speaker has just said but you want to move things on. This could be to summarize progress: "It's now 3.30pm; where are we …?" It could be to restate important points: "So let's confirm what we've agreed." Or, to be supportive: "That sounds like a good idea. Are we all happy with that proposal?"

■ When you do understand what the speaker has just said and you want to move on more deeply in a relationship. For example, some friends of mine were describing a problem in their village to the local member of parliament. The MP picked up on the fact that they were reticent to talk openly about their personal situations. He said, "Tell me more. I can see you're not telling me the full story. I need to see the big picture before I can recommend what action to take."

Don't be afraid to ask questions to get to the heart of the matter.

As they honestly and openly asked probing questions in an unaggressive way, they shared genuine perceptions about the present state of their industry. The result was an informal sharing of views about a potential project that eventually led to a product that was successfully launched onto the market.

Think strategically

It's a common situation: you're in a business meeting and have been there for an hour already, yet you haven't made significant progress on the real issues you wanted to address. This chapter discusses a range of approaches and techniques to help you think more strategically in a business setting. Sometimes you need to take a step back and think about different ways to tackle an issue, or think creatively and use analysis to move your thinking forward.

3.1

Take a step back

All too easily, you can be so close to your work that you lose focus on the real issues. This Secret looks at ways to help you keep focused on the overall aims and plan of action.

Here are some good, practical ways to help you think more strategically in business dealings.

■ **Clarify the aims.** Define the overall priorities and purposes, including underlying values and ethos.

■ **Create clear targets.** Set clear goals so that all those involved know precisely what they need to do and how to do it, and then break down these goals into smaller, manageable tasks.

■ **Ask the right questions.** Clarify the aim of what you are trying to solve in your own words.

case study There was a hotel that was losing money, but it was not until the consultant, Zee, came in that the manager realized how much. Zee challenged the manager and her staff to identify the basic cost to the hotel of a typical meal (breakfast and dinner), including food, drink, staff wages and other overheads. It

■ **Look for a wide range of solutions.** Gather information by undertaking new research and, as necessary, considering previous experience, the appropriate rules, procedures, etc., keeping an open mind and not judging ideas at this stage. Check your assumptions and, if necessary, challenge them.

■ **Encourage innovation.** Create an atmosphere in which all staff feel they can think and work in new ways, and therefore gain and retain customers more than your competitors.

■ **Make the right decisions.** They should be significant and objective and based on evidence that is well informed by sound information systems. Make a decision for the best available solution.

■ **Use the best criteria.** Identify the criteria to assess different options.

■ **Announce your decisions.** When you've made your decision, communicate the fact to all the people involved. It is not just about communicating information, but also making people feel included.

■ **Regularly review strategy.** Check what's happening with markets, products and customers. Keep questioning: "Why is this important?", "Why is this relevant?", "Why are we doing this?", so that fundamental issues are tackled.

Don't be afraid to ask such basic questions as "Why?", "Why is this important?", "Why are we doing this?"

took the bookkeeper and accountant a few weeks to work out the figure, since the financial systems were poor. Zee's recommendations included having fewer but better trained staff, more rigorous bookkeeping and accounting procedures and a much shorter menu that focused on more profitable meals.

3.2

Use de Bono's hats

The psychologist Edward de Bono wrote a book called *Six Thinking Hats* (1985), which encourages thinking and decision making from a range of difficult viewpoints.

De Bono's approach in this book can be summarized in the following six points, each with its own hat.

1 **The White Hat.** Look at the facts and information available as objectively as possible. Think about what gaps you have in your knowledge and try to fill them.

2 **The Red Hat.** Look at the subject from the point of view of our emotions. How do people feel about the issues? For example, are people angry or fearful of change? What are the instinctive responses?

case study Emotions were running high at a company's annual general meeting. The financial results were bad and the shareholders thought the company was poorly led and managed. By using the

3   **The Black Hat.** Look at the issues from a negative point of view. What is wrong with a plan? Why will it not work? What are the plan's disadvantages and risks?

4   **The Yellow Hat.** Look at the issue from a positive point of view. What is good and right about it? Why will the plan succeed? What are the plan's advantages and benefits? As Edward de Bono puts it, "This thinking … permits visions and dreams".

5   **The Green Hat.** Look at the issue from a creative point of view, seeing if there are different ways of generating fresh ideas.

6   **The Blue Hat.** Look at the issues from controlling the process of thinking and reaching decisions. This is needed by someone chairing or leading a meeting, to define the issue clearly.

Separate the subjective and emotional aspects of an issue from the objective facts to understand it more fully.

technique of the six hats, the chairman allowed expression of the various elements – factual, emotional, negative, positive, creative – and led the meeting clearly through to a constructive conclusion.

3.3

Hold an Appreciative Inquiry

A common way of solving problems is to focus on what to put right, possible causes of failures, and sometimes attributing blame to individuals. A more positive alternative to this is an approach that's known as an 'Appreciative Inquiry'.

An Appreciative Inquiry is different to the usual technique of problem solving in that it focuses on valuing existing people and systems ('appreciative') and exploring fresh possibilities for the future ('inquiry').

The five steps in an 'Appreciative Inquiry', each beginning with the letter D as a mnemonic device, are outlined opposite.

case study As managing director, Rob was keen to give a positive lead to his team, as he knew he had to introduce the idea of change in management to his colleagues. He followed the 'Appreciative Inquiry' approach. He defined the need to change as clearly as he could. In the 'discover' phase, he successfully enabled some managers to share with the wider

> **"A pessimist sees the difficulty in every opportunity; an optimist sees the opportunity in every difficulty"** Winston Churchill, British wartime leader

■ **Define.** Clarify the subject, problem or opportunity by defining it, as positively as you can.

■ **Discover.** Analyse what is good about current practices and what works well. Encourage colleagues to tell stories about their positive work experiences. Note the key points.

■ **Dream.** Build on what works well and creatively explore and imagine an even more ideal situation. One way of doing this is to brainstorm ideas (see Secret 4.1).

■ **Design.** Work out how the vision you have just dreamt might become a reality through new strategies to produce different systems and structures.

■ **Deliver.** Put into action the suggested design, keeping focused on the vision.

Build on what has worked well in the past and creatively explore even better ideas for the future.

group positive experiences that they had had in the company in the previous 10 years, which hardly any of the rest of the team knew about. So when it came to the dream stage, colleagues were encouraged and enthusiastic to explore new possibilities that built on good practice, some of which were then implemented through designing new systems in the company.

3.4

Apply random thinking

One useful method of creatively solving a problem when you are stuck is 'random thinking'. Here, as a basis to help you think creatively, you choose a noun that has nothing to do with the subject you are considering, and then see how that word's meaning can make a new and interesting connection.

The method is useful when you have run out of ideas thinking in a conventional way or when you need to break free from established ways of thinking. Choose a word that has no obvious connection with the problem you are trying to solve and see what links that word brings to mind. Words have very many associations and functions, and your brain may focus on one detail of a concept or a wider association.

case study The problem Dave and his colleagues were wrestling with was time management for middle managers. Three words came up using the 'random input' technique: 'colander', with its holes, which led to thinking that spare capacity was an important consid-

It is good to choose a concrete noun. You can do this by developing a list in advance of say 60 words and choosing one by looking at the time: if it is now 11.39, then choose noun number 39 on the list. Alternatively, consult a dictionary. This is what I did in the case study below: I looked at multiples of 13; page 130, p 260, p 390 and the 13th word (or the next one that is a noun). It is important to take the first aspect of a word that comes to mind, and have as few successive stages with 'this could mean that' as possible.

Choose a concrete noun at random and see what associations that word has to offer in terms of the problem you are trying to solve.

eration; 'lamp' suggested a need for innovation, understanding and illumination; 'stick' led to 'carrot and stick' – the need to give rewards for achieving goals. By using this technique, further lines of investigation were opened up which helped the group's thinking.

3.5

Take a PEST

A PEST analysis is an analysis of political, economic, social and technological changes. It helps you gain an overall view of the external influences that may affect your business and helps you see the way ahead – perhaps for a market you want to break into or if there are technological changes that may impact on your sphere of work.

Undertaking a PEST analysis means you will be able to identify the different factors that affect your business – they form the environment in which it exists. You will then be able to use these factors as a basis for your conclusions. It is especially helpful if you are working in a new market, such as a country you've not traded in before.

case study Before considering entering a new market for mobile phones, Gary's team undertook a PEST analysis. Politically, the telecommunications industry had recently been deregulated, allowing a much wider range of companies to operate than before. The economy was expanding, with younger consumers having higher disposable incomes. A significant social

A PEST analysis identifies:

■ **Political changes.** Deregulation of certain industries; changes in the government, laws, policy or regulations (e.g. imposition of trade tariffs); stability of government; possible conflict or war.

■ **Economic changes.** The state of the economy (growing or in recession); expanding markets; the effects of changes in the rate of inflation and interest rates; general taxation issues; levels of disposable income.

■ **Social changes.** Changes in population and demographic trends (changes in the number of births, deaths and marriages in a community over a period of time); social mobility; changes in types of employment; changes in lifestyle (e.g. more consumers buying ready-made meals).

■ **Technological changes.** The latest innovations; the effect of the Internet; increased working from home and lower unit costs because of technological factors.

By completing a PEST analysis you will see whether moving into a new market is likely to be profitable.

factor was a growing number of people living and working away from home and wanting to contact friends and family. Technologically, a new generation of mobile phones was about to be launched. By completing a PEST analysis, the team concluded that there was a significant market potential that was definitely worth exploring further.

3.6

Take a SWOT

Another important analysis will assess your strengths, weaknesses, opportunities and threats (a SWOT analysis). Do this and you will be better able to analyse the health of your business.

■ **Examine your strengths.** What does your business do better than anyone else? What do competitors in your trade see as your greatest strengths? What features are important in gaining and keeping your customers? What is your current financial position? What is your company's unique selling point (USP)?

■ **Examine your weaknesses.** What areas are you weak in and need to develop? What do competitors in your trade see as your weaknesses?

case study When Bill took over ownership of a local stationery-delivery company, he completed a SWOT analysis with his financial adviser. His strengths were that he had inherited a strong financial position from his predecessor and his company had a good reputation locally. Weaknesses were that his staff lacked skills and needed training, he held too much stock and the

What financial weaknesses do you have? Are you well-known for your business? Are your IT equipment and machinery up-to-date?

■ **Examine opportunities.** What trends are there in the market place – changes to people's lifestyles, new-product development and wider partnerships? Perhaps a competitor has recently gone bankrupt – could you take them over? Are there new market sectors you could pursue?

■ **Examine threats.** What problems do you currently find challenging? What are your competitors doing better than you? What effects might changes in IT, legislation, market demand or the economy have on your business?

Try to be as clear and definite as you can. For example, be more precise than "offers good value for money". Go through the different lists, putting the most important ones first.

Stop and look at the strengths, weaknesses, opportunities and threats of your business.

company's warehouse was poorly sited, just by a busy road junction. Opportunities were that a faster broadband was being installed to speed up orders. The threat came from an increasing number of competitors. By undertaking a SWOT analysis, Bill was able to gather information and use that as a basis for developing a strategy to move the business forward.

3.7

Harvest your thoughts

When you have looked at various ideas and have chosen to pursue one, you are left with those you rejected. The technique of harvesting is useful in that it applies and recycles the discarded ideas and methods to help you with other thinking processes.

Psychologist Edward de Bono developed harvesting as an approach to creative thinking. You can apply this process in your creative thinking by identifying the following:

case study The staff social club had become stuck in its ways and, at one of the regular meetings, the committee came up with ideas for new evening activities. Ultimately they decided on a bowling night out, but during the discussion other ideas were voiced, which were harvested rather than just left. Weekend breaks were an embryonic idea which two members of staff were asked to pursue. The discussion also

■ **Usable ideas.** Not only ideas that everyone recognizes as good but also others that could be taken up.

■ **Possible ideas.** Those ideas that seem impracticable – that cannot be put into practice easily – and are aspirational.

■ **Embryonic ideas.** These are the ideas that have potential but need to be developed further for the potential to be realized.

■ **Basic concepts and values.** Both those that have become clear during the discussion and those that were implicit but need to be made more explicit; also the broad approaches that are being adopted.

Also look to harvest from your discussions:

■ Ways of turning concepts into reality.
■ New focuses that need to be pursued specifically.
■ Changes from a certain way of thinking to a different way.
■ The general impression of the meeting of your creative thinking.

Don't reject any ideas; use possible ideas to reflect on your values and ethos and how you can turn those ideas into reality.

helped the club focus on their basic core values and ethos: in particular, the need to help new members of staff feel involved. The session, which was positive in tone, also noted that a change of thinking was required – to see new members of staff as an opportunity for fresh thinking. By adopting the harvesting technique, colleagues on the committee were able to feel positive about several ideas being taken forward, not just one.

Solve problems well

We all face problems at work. The key is to acknowledge them, know how to respond to them and make decisions that deal with them effectively. This chapter gives you techniques to develop wider thinking processes to help you form a fresh approach to problem solving: how you can respond creatively to difficulties, generate new ideas, examine causes and effects, identify the most important factors, and make overall evaluations of various options.

4.1

Generate fresh ideas

A well-established way of generating fresh ideas and developing new ways of thinking is brainstorming – holding a meeting at which colleagues suggest as many ideas as they can think of.

Brainstorming is a creative way of moving away from established thought patterns and developing new solutions to a problem. A leader is chosen who will facilitate (not direct) the meeting. First off, the facilitator or a colleague with specific knowledge of the issue clearly defines the problem, giving background details.

In responding to the problem that has been articualted, the participants should be encouraged to express themselves freely and

case study The team was considering new beauty products for consumers to buy as Christmas presents. They held a brainstorming session to discuss new ideas. Members of different departments were present – sales, marketing, product development – so that lessons learnt from previous years could be expressed. The facilitator led colleagues in brainstorming through a range of products, including shampoos and condi-

> "If the doors of perception were cleansed everything would appear to man as it is, infinite" **William Blake, English poet and artist**

widely. It is important that these ideas are not criticized or evaluated by others; the aim is to develop as many ideas as possible within a stated time. Obvious ideas should not be overlooked; and even crazy ideas may be suggested. The facilitator should write down the ideas on a flip chart. At the end, the team can establish criteria by which the best ideas can be developed further.

Effective brainstorming works best when colleagues build on one another's ideas and make creative connections between seemingly unconnected objects and processes.

Think of as many fresh ideas as possible within a certain time.

tioners, body lotions, aftershaves and deodorants. They looked at the state of the market and market trends, aims in selling new products and defined what may be meant by success. In their conclusions, they realized that their most useful time was spent considering precisely who would be the typical purchasers (women in their 20s) and who they would be buying for (their partners).

4.2

Examine causes and effects

Cause-and-effect analysis is one approach of using your mind to the full. It is an ordered way of analysing a problem and identifying possible causes so that you can deal with them effectively.

There are four key steps in cause-and-effect analysis:

1 Identify the problem as clearly as you can. Ask yourself the question words to guide you: 'who?', 'where?', 'when?', 'what?', 'how?' and 'why?'

case study Matt had been in the company for only a few weeks but he quickly felt under so much pressure that it was beginning to affect his work ... and his health. His manager did not seem to understand what was wrong and just pushed him all the more to achieve targets. The most difficult time was when Matt lost his temper with a major client. This came to the attention of his director who wisely sat down and considered the underlying effects of Matt's poor performance.

2 Consider all different aspects that relate to the problem. Some may be external, such as poor transport connections, some may be internal, such as staff feeling under pressure.

3 Analyse the effects of each of the different aspects in detail so that you clearly understand their importance.

4 Consider possible causes. Take each of the points in step 2, above, and identify as precisely as you can the possible causes. Brainstorming (see Secret 4.1) may help here. Take each of the possible causes in turn and keep on going back to identify the most fundamental causes.

You can also draw a flow chart, to show the series of steps that make up the stages of a process and the relationship between the causes and effects.

Stand back from a problem and see if it is caused by deeper, underlying matters, not yet resolved.

He discovered that the department in which Matt was working was, in fact, three members of staff short; it was also working with very out-of-date IT equipment, and that was causing them all to work more slowly than they otherwise would. By identifying and working on the root causes, Matt's director was able to recruit and train further members of staff and order new IT equipment. Not only did Matt's work improve, but so too did his department's morale.

4.3

Apply the Pareto principle

When having to use your mind to make decisions about solving problems, you need to identify the key factors or issues and tackle these.

One key to identifying the most important factors is known as the Pareto principle, or the 80/20 rule. The expression is named after the Italian economist and sociologist Vilfredo Federico Pareto (1848-1923), who formulated this principle. It is seen, for example, in company sales: 80% of sales may come from 20% of customers. The

case study Managers at the mail-order distribution centre wanted to deal with customer complaints about goods being returned. They collected data and quickly realized that 85% of the problems of returns were due to two key issues: the goods were defective or they were not the items the customers had originally ordered. More minor problems making up the remaining 15% of complaints were that the goods were damaged during delivery by the distributor, that the

"Eighty percent of the land in Italy is owned by twenty percent of the people"

Vilfredo Federico Pareto, economist

Pareto principle can also be applied to problem solving: as you analyse all the relevant causes of a problem, assess their relative importance. You will probably discover that 80% of the problems are caused by 20% of the contributing factors. If you can deal with these 20% of the causes effectively, then you are more likely to be successful overall. This principle is based on the fact that it is inefficient and unproductive to tackle the relatively insignificant factors.

Make a positive decision to deal with the most important issues, not all possible factors.

packages were not accepted at the address given or were addressed incorrectly. The managers realized that, to be most effective, they should concentrate on the two key issues of defective goods and wrongly ordered items. By identifying these factors, they were able to develop solutions to reduce their effects as far as they could, so dealing efficiently with a greater number of complaints than they might have done if they had tried to deal with the whole range of issues.

4.4

Evaluate the pros and cons

When you have to choose between different options, following the technique of evaluating the pros and cons can be helpful in guiding you to come to the right decision.

As you consider the various possibilities from which you need to choose, go through the following six steps.

1 Firstly, make a list. Write down all the different options that are available to you.

2 List the different advantages of pursuing each particular course of action; the results of making a certain decision, etc.

3 List the disadvantages of pursuing that particular course of action; the results of making a certain decision, etc.

4 Go back over your lists and make sure you have included all the possible implications, results and risks of your action or decision that you can think of. You may realize that some of the factors may be non-negotiable.

"Nothing is more difficult, and therefore more precious, than to be able to decide" **Napoleon Bonaparte**

5 It may be clear at this point which action you should decide to follow. As you have thought about the issues and have written down the different points, the way may have become clearer in your mind. If this is not so, then look again at the different items in each list and give a particular value to each. Write a number indicating a certain relative worth you give that item: minus values for disadvantages (-1 for slightly disadvantageous to -5 for very disadvantageous); positive values for advantageous (+1 for slightly advantageous to +5 for very advantageous). For example, if you are considering launching a new product, long-term profitability may be more important than the effects on your existing resources, so you could put +5 by long-term profitability and -1 by the effects on your existing resources.

6 Once you have written numbers of relative values by the side of the different options, add up the scores to guide you in your decision making.

Weigh up the advantages and disadvantages of each option before making your decision.

4.5

Respond creatively to problems

We've all had times when our thinking has come to a road block and we simply cannot solve a problem. That's when we need to look at innovative ways to tackle the challenge.

Here's some guidance on creative ways to help you resolve difficulties.

■ **Talk to colleagues.** Talk to them; don't email them. Explain the difficulty to them with as little jargon as possible and as simply as you can. Get them to ask you to define the heart of the problem. Discuss

---

case study Jane was asked to act as consultant to a restaurant manager who was trying to improve his business. Rather than asking the manager to think directly about ways of making the restaurant better, Jane suggested asking the opposite question as a creative way of looking at this issue. So she asked the manager to consider the factors that would make his restaurant the worst in the city. They came up with the

---

it, not only to clarify it but also to work on creative ways to help you through it. Listen to them … really listen (see Secrets 2.7 to 2.9).

■ **Consult an expert.** Talk to someone who has dealt with a similar problem before. He or she may suggest looking at the matter from an angle that is different to the one you had already thought of.

■ **Re-draw the problem.** Think of different ways of describing a problem. Literally draw it, or think of a way of describing it using art, music or drama.

■ **Look at the bigger issue.** If you are stuck on an issue, perhaps that is not the underlying one; broaden it out and ask a wider question, "What are the causes of that issue?"

■ **Dig deep.** Aim at solving the underlying, not the surface, issue. If you are launching a new product, don't be vague about what constitutes success. Ask yourself, "What would success look like in specific terms?"

■ **Make a pattern diagram.** Secret 1.6 will help you think outside the box. Use a dictionary or thesaurus to generate associated ideas, words and phrases. Look at related words and opposites.

■ **Sleep on it.** Take a break… sometimes it really helps to leave the problem for a while and come back to it later.

Think of different ways of describing a problem. Re-draw it, literally.

following: tasteless and expensive food, poor location, no parking nearby, unclean facilities, no atmosphere, poor value for money, unfriendly staff who were rude and knew nothing about the menu, intrusive music, bad decoration, and no air-conditioning. After identifying these key factors, Jane was able to apply these results in discussing possible ways of improving the restaurant with the manager.

Develop your memory

We all have difficulty remembering things to do, people's names, people to contact, points to mention in a conversation or email, or important numbers and dates. This chapter explores a range of techniques to help you develop your memory to recall such matters. As you read through these various methods, you will find that some ways work better for you than others. Choose and develop the ways for remembering that work for you.

5.1

Refresh your memory

We all find it difficult to remember things … names, faces, numbers, the key points of a speech, things to buy in the supermarket. And the older we become, the more the difficulty seems to worsen. How can you improve your memory?

Here are some key ways of help improve your memory:

■ **Form a connection.** Make a connection in your mind between what you are trying to remember and something else with which you are already familiar.

■ **Make it distinctive.** Choose something strange, unusual, humorous or exaggerated to help you associate the two things. Think of some of the surreal paintings by Salvador Dali. Be imaginative and creative.

■ **Be particular.** Choose something specific rather than general.

■ **Close to home.** Choose something meaningful for you and your life experiences – something that's almost part of you. What you choose has to work for you, not necessarily for anyone else.

one minute wonder Suppose you are trying to remember a woman's name; she's called Davina. When you first met her, she was wearing a yellow T-shirt. You associate in your mind 'Davina' with a yellow object you are already familiar with and can visualize easily – a daffodil, say. You can then use that visual link to trigger the memory and help you to successfully recall her name, Davina.

■ **Clear, bold signals.** Choose colours such as red for 'stop', green for 'go'; and symbols such as √ for 'yes', X for 'no'.

■ **Strong visual images.** Choose concrete, rather than abstract, images, and three-dimensional as well as two. Choosing positive and nice images works better than choosing negative or bad ones.

■ **Make up a rhyme.** When I first learnt German, our teacher taught us a rhyme to help us with the beginning of words that could not be separated from the main verb; I still remember the rhyme 40 years later.

■ **Use acronyms.** Make up a word from the first letters of something (acronym) you need to remember (see Secret 5.2).

■ **Group things.** Put items to remember in categories. If you have to remember several items to get in a supermarket, for example, group them according to fruit, meat, toiletries and so on.

Make a connection between what you are trying to remember and something you know well.

5.2

Use mnemonics

Mnemonic devices are used to aid the memory, and there are two key types that you can employ to help your ability to recall information: mnemonic phrases or sentences and acronyms.

■ **Acronyms.** An acronym is a word that uses the first letter of each word in a phrase or sentence to make another word. They are often used for organizations, such as UNESCO (United Nations Educational, Scientific and Cultural Organization) or NASA (National Aeronautics and Space Administration). They are used as an abbreviation, primarily, but you can also use acronyms as an easy way to help you remember something – PEST analysis, for example, which stands for Political, Economic, Social and Technological analysis (Secret 3.5).

■ **Mnemonic phrases.** A mnemonic sentence is created solely for the purpose of remembering specific information that's usually unrelated to the sentence. It is best understood by an example, such as this one, which recalls the order of the traditional planets: "My Very Energetic Mother Just Served Us Nine Pizzas" (Mercury, Venus, Earth, Mars, Jupiter, Saturn, Uranus, Neptune, Pluto). Another example is "All Cows Eat Grass" for A, C, E, G, the musical notes represented by the four spaces in the bass clef.

one minute wonder Think of a short number sequence, such as a code or telephone number, that you need to memorize. Now create a sentence in which the number of letters for each word form the digits of the number. The more unusual, personal, creative, visually strong the sentence, the easier it will be to remember. For example, 12166 could be "I am a memory device" or, better still, "I am a yellow banana", which is a more memorable phrase.

Acronyms and mnemonic phrases are very useful ways of remembering information in sequences, especially in the short term. Being, by background, a dictionary writer, I use these a lot when having to remember a few key words when I have to lead a presentation. For example, on my course on report writing, I teach the basic elements of 'STAIR', which stands for 'Scope; Target audience; Analysis; Interpretation; Recommendations'.

■ **Remembering numbers.** You can also apply this technique to remembering numbers. For example, suppose you had to remember 4716 and 2459. you could make up a sentence consisting of one word with four letters, followed by one with 7, one with 1 and one with 6. How about, "Ravi Shankar I admire"? Then you need a sentence consisting of a 2 letter word, followed by one with 4 , 5 and then 9 letters. How about, "He eats every Wednesday"?

If you have to remember a short list of words, use an acronym or strong mnemonic phrase.

5.3

Use the link system

The link system is a way of remembering a series of items, such as a list of words. It is an imaginative way that uses the power of your creativity.

The link system is a powerful technique that uses visual images in a story to remember a list. With the link system, we associate a word or another item in a list with some of the pictures, images or notions connected with it. As I have mentioned before, it is important to make your images strange, unusual, humorous, exaggerated or distinctive in some way in order to make them more memorable. You are replacing an ordinary item you need to remember by something more memorable. So it can help if the image is larger or more exaggerated than reality. Adding movement is also very useful.

Here are a couple of examples to give you an idea of how this method can work to help your memory:

Example One

This morning I walked to our local convenience store and had to remember to buy several items: washing-up liquid, yoghurt, bananas and some crisps. The way I chose to remember these items was to visualize myself in a scenario: I am jogging (jog rhymes with the 'yog' of yoghurt) along the pavement, sliding around on the thick gooey surface (washing-up liquid), bending my body (in a banana shape – I could add wearing a yellow top reading Yellow pages, for good measure), before I reach the shop, only to find that it is burnt down (burnt to a crisp, which it really was a few years ago).

Example Two

At a party I was introduced to five people in short succession. I decided to use the link system to remember their names: Lance, Shelley, Jack, Deborah and Sean. I quickly came up with a scene in my mind, which began with Lance. I associated the name with Lance Armstrong, the cyclist, so I imagined him on a bike – a tandem, in fact, with actress Shelley Winters on the back. They were being chased by a man with an axe (Jack Nicholson in *The Shining*) towards Deborah Kerr on a clifftop (a scene from the film *Black Narcissus*). Munching grass on the cliff and ignoring everyone else was the cartoon character Sean the Sheep, one of my children's favourites.

These examples no doubt seem convoluted and strange, but, because the images and references meant something to me, they had the desired effect in each case and I remembered all the items and names that I needed to.

Associate an ordinary item you need to remember with something more unusual, exaggerated, or distinctive.

5.4

Replace words with a picture

When you come across an abstract word or phrase, it is useful to think of something visual that can help you to recall that word or phrase.

A few years ago, I was working with a colleague who couldn't remember how to spell the word 'assume' until she came up with a humorous way to remember the spelling. She said it made an "<u>ass</u> of <u>u</u> (you) and <u>me</u>". Easy! By replacing something abstract, such as a spelling, with a more concrete, vivid picture, the task becomes simpler.

Remember that the visual image you choose must work for you. Other people cannot impose their ideas on you; the pictures must ring true in your own experience.

---

case study Stuart had to give a short, five-minute presentation to his colleagues on how his department had come to develop new products. He didn't want to write down the text but wanted to remember his four key points: Background, Ideas, Research and Decisions.

Other ideas to help you remember words or phrases:

■ **Place names.** Certain place names can trigger memories. For example, I associate the town of Crewe with a railway junction, which I've passed through on many occasions, so whenever I meet someone from Crewe or see an address from there I think of railways.

■ **Numbers.** The shape of numbers suggests visual triggers too. The numeral 2, for example, is shaped like a swan, while 8 is shaped like an hourglass.

■ **Foreign words.** The German for 'town hall' is *rathaus*. To remember it, I think of a Pied-Piper-of-Hamelin style town hall with rats infesting the building. Another example is the Mandarin Chinese word for 'journey': *yělù*. I think of a group of faithful pilgrims who are singing 'O Come All <u>Ye</u> Faithful' on their way to the <u>loo</u> (toilet).

■ **Names.** A friend has two sons: Paul and Leo. Leo is the younger and shorter, so I remember 'L': little Leo.

Replace something abstract that you need to remember by a visual image that rings true in your own experience.

These four points could be abbreviated to a simple acronym BIRD. All he then had to do was visualize a picture of a bird and he could easily recall the four key points. He was, therefore, able to make the presentation without the need for written notes to guide him.

5.5

Imagine a journey

Another useful memory aid is to imagine that you
are making a journey. Then picture points along that
journey and associate items that you want to
remember with each point. By doing so, you should
be able to remember several different items.

I've lived in the house where I'm currently living for 27 years.
I've worked from home for all that time and usually go out for a walk
round the block before work in the morning and at lunchtime. My
walk passes several particular locations:

■ A postbox on the corner of two streets.
■ Mrs Johnson's house, a lady I've got to know over the years.
■ A busy main road.
■ A convenience store.
■ A local primary school which both my children went to.
■ The local Chinese takeaway, whose owner Chas, I know.
■ A new block of flats.
■ Sally's house – I sometimes see her walking her dog in the morning.

All these items are entrenched in my memory: some have long
and emotional memories associated with them (such as the school,
where I was a school governor for several years).

If my task is to remember several items, I can do this by associating a certain aspect of each item I want to remember with a particular stage on the journey:

■ **Postbox.** The letter I need to post.

■ **Mrs Johnson's house.** The birthday card I need to send today (it's nearly November, the month of Mrs Johnson's birthday).

■ **The busy main road.** The railway magazine I want to buy (busy main railway line, busy main road).

■ **The convenience shop.** The eggs I need to buy.

■ **The primary school.** The study and preparation I've got to do for a talk I'm giving on Sunday.

■ **The Chinese takeaway.** A reminder to phone a friend in Hong Kong (where Chas, the owner of the takeaway, comes from).

■ **The new block of flats.** A reminder to clean the kitchen floor so it looks and smells new.

■ **Sally as she walks her dog.** A reminder to check on details of a walking holiday we're planning.

Associating items with steps on a journey is an effective memory tool.

5.6

Think of a story

A further way to remember and recall a series of items is to use a narrative technique. Simply make up a story that links all the items together.

My wife enjoys story-telling evenings with friends. She takes a bag with memorable objects in it, and these act as triggers to her memory to tell the story. You can use this technique and make up a story that helps you remember a list of things. By choosing certain items in a particular order, you will be able to remember the various items associated with the objects in that particular order.

For example, here is a list of objects that form the triggers for the story that follows:

- a bell
- a paperweight
- an atlas
- a dried flower

"The **doorbell** rang (a reminder to buy batteries for my digital camera). It was the postman who I noticed was carrying a very heavy bag of mail (**paperweight**: a reminder to phone the local stationer's to ask them to deliver more paper). He had a parcel for me. It had lots of colourful foreign stamps on it (idea of heaviness and touch and a strong visual cue of seeing him weighed down) which I'll give to a friend who collects stamps. I opened the parcel. It was an old **atlas** (a reminder to enquire about a trip to Thailand we're planning for next year) that I had ordered for another friend as a birthday present. As I flicked through the old musty (sense of smell) pages, I noticed that inside the pages was an old pressed **dried flower**, which I lifted up to my nose to smell to detect if it still had any scent (use of different senses; a reminder to buy flowers for my wife)."

Well, as a story it probably won't win any prizes, but as an aid to remembering it contains lots of useful material. It uses objects with strong associations for me, action (such as unwrapping a parcel), colour to intensify the visual images, sound (the bell) and smell too – that way the story can work with all the senses to reinforce the memories.

By thinking up different parts of a story, you will be able to remember a series of items.

5.7

Remember key phrases in a talk

The most important thing about trying to remember a speech or presentation is to remember its key points, not every detail.

When giving a talk without notes, I plan a careful three-point structure:

1 **Introduction – with one key thought.**

2 **Several key messages.**

3 **Conclusion – with one key thought.**

I plan and work very carefully on the exact words I choose in the introduction (in order to catch my listeners' attention) and in the conclusion (because these are the final words I will leave with my listeners). I work very hard to choose certain precise phrases that will lift the occasion. I don't, however, usually plan my opening words, "Good morning", "Hello" etc – I leave that to the actual situation when I can gauge the mood of the audience.

Coming to the central part of my presentations, I don't plan each part in detail. I do not plan every sentence meticulously, only the key phrases. Take that last sentence, for example: the key words and phrases were "not plan", "sentence meticulously", "key phrases"; not "I", "do", "every", "only", "the". In that sentence I would try to remember the phrases "sentence meticulously" and "key phrases", and make sure that I spoke these out clearly.

Another key way of communicating is to use synonyms (words with a similar meaning to a particular word, such as 'large' and 'big'). So, if I am saying "thank you" to someone on a formal occasion, I will use the words "thank you" but I will also elaborate on that and use synonyms for thank you: "express our appreciation", "we are grateful" or "gratitude". For example: "We appreciate all you have done for us over the years and want to express our gratitude to you." But I only have to remember "thank you". Synonyms are like repeating the same content, which is a common method that teachers use.

In your preparation for a talk, concentrate on memorizing the key phrases.

5.8

Remember names

Many of us find it difficult to remember people's names. We recognize a familiar face and want to greet the person with their name but find that it escapes us.

Here are a few tips on how to remember names:

■ **Prepare yourself.** Be mentally alert when you ask someone's name and listen very closely. Concentrate on the sounds of the name as the person says it.

■ **Use repetition.** Don't be afraid to ask someone to repeat their name: "I'm sorry, I didn't quite catch that?" You could always say the name back to the person to check that you have pronounced it right. The more you repeat the name, the more likely you are to remember it.

■ **Write down names .** I find this helpful. As soon as I meet someone new and have found out their name I try to write it down. If you don't know how to spell their name, you can write it using a phonetic (or your own spelling) system. Putting it down on paper will help you remember it. Of course you need to do this unobtrusively and out of sight of the person concerned. It can be done easily in meetings.

■ **Use people's names when addressing them.** "Thanks, Peter, that's very helpful." Beware of overdoing this, though: to use someone's name every time you speak to them is excessive.

■ **Be realistic.** If you are joining a new organization, you can be overwhelmed by having to learn the names of every other person. What is realistic, however, is to learn the name of one new person each day.

■ **Associate a feature with a particular image.** If Brenda is blonde, you can think of 'B' for both blonde and Brenda. Notice the person's hairstyle, nose, teeth, smile, eyebrows or cheeks. An acquaintance has slightly protruding upper teeth, so I think of dental and Dave. The face of a man at a conference reminded me of a Coca Cola bottle, so I used that to remember his name, Mr Coles (<u>Cola</u>/<u>Coles</u>).

■ **Locate the name and person.** Think of where you are meeting that person for the first time. That will help you when you recognize a face but forget the person's name. The place you are seeing them in is different from where you originally met them, so think of '<u>Brian</u> who you met in the <u>bank</u>', for example.

■ **Use an order.** Put names in alphabetical order in your mind. This is a personal one, as I write dictionaries, but, if I have Julie, June and Karen sitting next to each other in a presentation I am giving, then I put their names in that order.

Actively concentrate as you meet someone for the first time when they tell you their name.

5.9

Remember numbers

These days there are so many numbers to remember, such as bank PINs and entry codes for offices. How do we remember them all?

Here are some few tips on how to remember numbers:

■ **Break down a long number.** Break a large number into smaller series of digits. So: 4677931 could become 46 77 93 1.

■ **Remember the difficult bits.** In the UK, for example, all mobile numbers begin with 07, so you don't really need to remember that. Use your memory for the difficult parts.

■ **Use rhymes.** Divide a long number up into shorter chunks and then make a rhyme of these. A friend's phone number is 525210, so I think of singing '52-52-10'.

■ **Look for patterns.** Seek patterns and associations for you. For example, I was born in 1952 and our area telephone code is 01865, so anything with those patterns or very similar (say, 52 or 865) are more easily memorable for me.

■ **Other associations.** Here are some other common associations for numbers: 10 Downing Street; 12 tribes of Israel/disciples; 13 beginning of teenage years; 16 ('sweet sixteen' for a girl); 18 (year of adulthood); 19th hole (for bar of a golf club); 20/20 vision; *Catch-22*; Psalm 23 in *The Bible* ('The Lord is my shepherd'); 24 hours in a day;

The 39 Steps; 42 (ultimate answer to questions of the universe as in *The Hitchhiker's guide to the Galaxy*); 57 Heinz varieties; Route 66, the famous US highway; 144 is a dozen dozens; 666, the number of the beast in *The Bible*; 1066, when William the Conqueror and the Normans invaded Britain; 1492, as remembered with the rhyme, "In fourteen hundred and ninety-two, Columbus sailed the ocean blue"; 1914, the beginning of the First World War; 1918, end of the First World War; 1939, beginning of the Second World War; 1945, end of Second World War; 1947, the year India gained independence from the UK; 1984, the title of George Orwell's novel *Nineteen Eighty-four*.

Devise 'pegs' that stand for digits or numbers. One is:

0	snow/yo-yo
1	sun/bun
2	shoe
3	tree
4	door
5	hive
6	bricks/sticks
7	heaven
8	gate
9	wine/line

So, to remember 4316, you can think of looking through a **door** at a **tree** in the **sun** in a house made of **bricks** in the background. Some people find this rhyming system helpful.

To remember numbers, break them up if they are long, create associations for them and use rhymes.

5.10

Remember dates

Certain dates, such as birthdays and wedding anniversaries, are important in our everyday lives. If you forget such events you will find yourself in an unfortunate position with those around you.

Ways of remembering dates include the following:

■ **Fix the month.** Associate the month at least with some major festival, such as Christmas or St Patrick's Day (17th March).

■ **Associate the date with a memory.** Associate something you can remember with the particular day. For example, my wife's birthday is 25 November and my daughter's is 27 November. I occasionally get them confused, until I remember that before our daughter was born, friends kept on asking my wife whether the baby might be born on her birthday. That's how I remember that she was not born before, but after, my wife's birthday.

> **case study** I once worked with a colleague whose name was June, and during the course of our working together I had to write an informal report on our joint response to a project. I started a paragraph in the

■ **Use rhymes and word play.** Make up a rhyme for a particular month and use one of the techniques in Secret 5.9 to remember the number of the day. For example, "It will soon be sunny June", and "sun, sun" (one, one) could recall the date 11th of June.

■ **Link the time of year to a personality trait.** A friend, Alex, has a lovely energetic character, so that reminds me that his birthday is in spring (April) – also alliteration (using the same letter at the beginning of a word) for Alex and April helps.

■ **Don't try to remember all of them!** Write them down instead. Set automatic reminders in your diary and scheduling software for regular tasks – bills due on a certain day each month; remembering important birthdays (put a note in advance, as well as on the day!); renewing insurance, etc. I personally keep a birthday book and write all new birthdays in that. Part of my end-of-year routine is to transfer birthdays to the appropriate dates in my diary for the coming year.

■ **Don't rely on your memory or electronic reminder.** It's a good idea to always keep a hard-copy record of the most important dates you need to remember.

Use word associations and written reminders to remember dates.

report, "May June and I (or should that be May, June and July?)". So the month of June is memorable for me in that way. This funny incident helps me remember events that take place in June.

Focus your mind

This chapter could revolutionize life in offices throughout the world! Too often we're distracted from our work, blaming others when things go wrong, while remaining insecure within ourselves. This chapter is all about focusing your mind: concentrating your attention on your work to do the best you possibly can, taking responsibility and becoming confident, coura-geous, positive and enthusiastic, while at the same time remaining realistic about the challenges of life.

6.1

Concentrate better

Sometimes you need to give undivided attention to a particular piece of work that requires your full attention. How do you do that?

■ **Find a quiet space.** Find an empty office in your department, work from home for the day or come in early so that you can work undisturbed if you need to.

■ **Set up your environment to suit you.** Do your best to control your working environment. Some people enjoy having music in the background, as it aids their concentration, while others need complete quiet to work well.

■ **Make thorough preparations.** Gather all the information you need before you begin your concentrated work. This process of gathering

case study Harshad says: "I always arrive at the office at 7am. It's fairly quiet then, so I can get on with writing tasks that really matter. Like yesterday, for instance: I had to finish a business proposal and needed quality time for clear thinking. It was important that I worked

can take place during periods that require less concentration. It is an inefficient use of your time – and troublesome – to have to use your precious concentration time to undertake routine practical tasks.

■ **Reserve your most productive time.** Know what time of day you work best and guard that time so that you do your most productive work then.

■ **Leave mundane tasks for other times.** Do your routine work in times that don't need your full concentration.

■ **Reward yourself.** If necessary, give yourself a reward so that you have something to look forward to after your concentrated period.

■ **Recharge your batteries.** Give yourself a 10-minute break after 50 minutes. This will allow your mind to process and digest your thoughts and you may find yourself solving some of the problems raised during your time of concentrated action.

Know what time of day you work best and guard that time as far as possible.

through logically in my mind all the different aims and priorities we wanted to set as a company. I needed some peace and quiet to focus my attention so that I could concentrate fully on it and not get distracted by the normal office interruptions."

6.2

Become more confident

In business, you need to focus your mind and personality on being confident and bold, knowing you have the drive to succeed in your quests and achieve what you want.

Here are some ways to help you become more confident:

■ **Think positive.** Rather than complaining about not being confident and turning in on yourself, determine to be positive. Concentrate on the positive elements of work, problems to be solved, your life and your attributes. See also Secret 6.5.

■ **Recognize your own personality.** Listen to friends, of course, but don't be overwhelmed by them. You are a distinct individual with your own personal character.

■ **Develop your character.** Aim high – aim for honesty and integrity as far as you are able.

> **"Boldness in business is the first, second, and third thing"**

Thomas Fuller (1654–1734), English physician and writer

■ **Develop your own skills.** Don't stand still. Be determined to stand out from the crowd. For example, if you need training in giving presentation skills, then go on a course that will help you improve them.

■ **Believe in yourself.** Think about and take pride in who you are and what you are doing. If you're a salesman trying to sell something you don't believe in, it will show. You need to be convinced about the kind of person you are and the skills, gifts and work you can offer.

■ **Prepare well.** Remember the saying, "If you fail to prepare, you prepare to fail". Do a good job at your thinking and research before a presentation. Work hard at the background material. Do you remember the picture of a duck calmly moving across a pond, while underneath it is paddling furiously? Don't neglect the background work – understand new techniques; check out how things work.

■ **Target problem areas.** Work on the aspects of your life and work that you are scared of. Don't concentrate on the negative, though; focus on the positives. Visualize yourself as confident, and that is one step to becoming so. Become the change you want to be.

Focus your mind and whole self on those areas of your life where you lack confidence, and inject some positivity.

6.3

Build up courage

Courage is not the absence of fear; courage is doing something even when you have fears. This means that you have to combat fear to take action in spite of reservations that might otherwise hold you back.

Here are some ways to help you find more courage; they are all designed to help you move on and grow as a person:

■ **First learn to accept fears.** Some fears are healthy – like being afraid of touching a hot cooker. They are natural physical responses. Accept that we all have them but sometimes need to overcome them.

■ **Be kind to yourself.** A close friend was recently in a car accident and lost confidence in driving. We all have setbacks and need to learn to

case study Mark was an aspiring leader so he was eagerly looking forward to going on a leaders' conference. He was particularly struck by the motivational talk at the close of the event. The speaker said that the two most important aspects of leadership were skills and integrity. The speaker's final statement was that if he had to choose only one aspect it would be integrity.

accept them and adapt to them. His solution was to sign up for a refresher driving course. This led on to a further course in advanced skills, which gave him the confidence to return to the road.

■ **Think objectively.** Write down your five worst fears. Which of them has actually happened? How likely are they to happen or recur? What is the worst that could happen? Writing down our fears and thinking about them rationally often serves to 'tame' them, making them feel less alarming.

■ **Don't let your fears get the better of you.** If you're scared of standing up and speaking to a large group of colleagues, practise with a smaller group, or even with just one other person to begin with. Get response to build up confidence in what you're saying. With that confidence, you'll develop the courage to take it to a wider audience.

■ **Turn things round.** Turn the obstacles that come into your mind into opportunities. Don't say 'but' and focus on the negatives; say 'and' and focus on the positives. Don't fixate on the problem; look at it with the aim of improving or solving the situation. You are the positive force.

Don't let your fears get the better of you. Remember that we all have fears that we learn to overcome.

He commented that this may not always 'pay' in the short run, but it would in the long run. Mark immediately thought of colleagues who he knew had had the courage to leave an organization because that organization's practices were not always legal and they did not think they could retain their integrity as long as they remained working there.

6.4

Take responsibility

"Life is difficult" are the opening words of M. Scott Peck's *The Road Less Traveled*; hard things happen beyond our control. But the issue is not what has happened in the past but how we respond to difficulties in life and take responsibility for our lives.

So, how can we take responsibility for our lives?

■ **You cannot change what's already happened.** It's easy to spend time thinking, "if only such and such hadn't happened". But you need to accept the fact that you can't change the past.

■ **Move beyond the blame factor.** There's a time and a place for naming, shaming and blaming people – but we don't have to do that all the time. If we move beyond the blame factor of what happened in the past, we can think out what responsibilities we can take for the present and future. Think about what this means in terms of your present business context.

■ **Become the change you want to be.** It's about us changing who we are. That may take courage. One way is to visualize the person you want to be and then think how different you are at the moment from that person. What can you do to make the images cohere?

> **"**The ancient Romans had a tradition: whenever one of their engineers constructed an arch, as the capstone was hoisted into place, the engineer assumed accountability for his work in the most profound way possible; he stood under the arch**"**

Michael Armstrong, former CEO of AT&T

■ **Overcome difficulties.** Two friends of mine have children with severe special needs. In each case, the parents have had great difficulties in securing the best education for their children but they have all become stronger people as a result of what they have experienced.

■ **Don't sweat the small stuff.** All too often I get wound up over small details and minor inconveniences at work. I'm learning that life is just too important for me to allow these things to overwhelm me.

■ **Be positive.** Do something helpful for others.

■ **Work at your business relationships.** Communicate less by email and more by face-to-face contact. If working relationships are good, you can achieve so much more. The saying about TEAMwork is true: Together Everyone Achieves More.

Move beyond apportioning blame so you can think about what responsibilities you can take for the future.

6.5

Be positive

Some people's minds are negative. Their thoughts are preoccupied with problems and difficulties. Other people are neutral, always 'sitting on the fence' and never really getting behind anything. Instead of either of these attitudes, cultivate a positive, enthusiastic outlook: you will discover that it works wonders!

Here are some tips on ways to be more positive:

■ **Aim high.** Do the small tasks that you have to do well – no, don't just do them well, do them as best as you possibly can. Don't settle for doing an average job, or even a good job, but do your very best. Your hard work will be noticed.

■ **Take opportunities.** I recently was asked to do a radio interview on a book I'd written that had just been published. At first I said no, and

> **case study** Louise recently decided to give up smoking. She used nicotine patches to aid the process. She had to start at step 1, where the patches contained high nicotine levels. After four weeks she moved to

later changed my mind. (I'd had a bad experience during a live interview once and had determined to do only recorded interviews in future.) I reflected on my decision and realized that it made sense to do the interview, regardless of my feelings of reservation.

■ **Keep trying.** Remember the proverb, "If at first you don't succeed, then try, try again". Such a mentality is essential in business.

■ **Prepare for the future.** Work not only for the present but also have one eye on where you want to be in five years' time (do you remember being asked that at your interview?). Well, break down the pathway to your goal into tasks that you can do this month, this week, today. "The journey of a thousand miles begins with a single step" (Lao Tzu).

■ **Work at the big picture... and the small details.** Maybe you're a 'big picture' person? Well, don't ignore the small details of life. Stop and thank someone who gives you good service. Conversely, if you're someone who gets immersed in the fine detail in life, deliberately stand back and look at the bigger picture – see how far you've already come ... as well as how far you've got to go.

Work to develop a positive, optimistic attitude: you will find it uplifting!

step 2, where the patches contained lower nicotine levels, and eventually finished step 3, so becoming a non-smoker. By working out and taking small, manageable steps, she became the person she wanted to be.

Inspire your mind

The English statesman, prime minister and novelist Benjamin Disraeli said, "Nurture your mind with great thoughts, for you will never go any higher than you think". Your mind is key to your working life, so you need to take good care of it. In this final chapter we explore how this will help you become successful. We'll also look at ways to reduce stress in our lives, keep our minds open to new ideas and consider how we can work most effectively.

Mindpower **secrets**

7.1

Balance the work-life ratio

It is vital that you find ways to help you manage and reduce stress at work. Life should never be all about work; if it is, you need to reset the work-life balance.

Here are some guidelines to help you succeed, not only in your work but also more generally in your life:

■ **Schedule rest.** Make regular time slots (in your diary if necessary) for rest. And plan ahead: if you know you've got a busy week coming up, try to make the weekends either side, or the following week, less busy.

case study In Ron's first eight years of working independently, he overworked; his job basically took over his life. He spent some time with his wife and children but was too focused on his work. The result was that stress gradually built up and he realized he needed to seek professional help. He sought medical advice, and had to learn to build a more regular, balanced lifestyle. So Ron developed regular habits of

■ **Don't say yes to everything.** Learn to say no (see Secret 7.4) and don't try to control everything: set yourself realistic goals.

■ **Plan holidays in advance.** A colleague plans a special event, such as a weekend away, every 6 weeks or so. By doing so he always has something to look forward to that's never far away.

■ **Family time.** Schedule in regular blocks of time for having fun with your partner and family.

■ **Take up a new hobby or voluntary work.** Helping a local charity and working with other people in your neighbourhood will take you out of yourself.

■ **Time with friends.** Spend time relaxing with friends; these are the people you can share a joke with, and a sense of humour is important.

■ **Engage in physical exercise.** Jogging, cycling, swimming, walking or dancing – physical exercise of some sort is vital to your wellbeing.

■ **Have fun.** Make sure you do something you enjoy every day.

■ **Watch what you eat and drink.** Eat a good breakfast and health snacks. Avoid too much caffeine. Cut down on cigarettes and alcohol. Reduce your intake of sugar and fat. Don't eat heavy meals late at night.

Some stress is inevitable; the question is what will you do differently to help keep stress levels manageable?

walking around the block (5, 10, 20, 40 minutes, depending on the time available) and intentionally developing a support group of friends who he met with regularly. The result was that, although he sometimes still became stressed, he became more resilient and had in place coping mechanisms to help him deal with stress more effectively than he had previously been able to.

7.2

Achieve in a team

In reducing stress and working well together with colleagues in a team, a vital step is to clarify roles and responsibilities. That way each person knows what he or she is expected to do. This reduces stress and makes for better communication.

Ways to work better with colleagues in a team include:

■ **Show appreciation.** Learn to be positive about the various skills and emphases of different members of the team. Attitudes are important. Respect one another.

■ **Keep everyone in the picture.** Communicate as much as you can about your joint goals and aims to build a team outlook. Give clear instructions – explain why you're doing something, so that colleagues can see the bigger picture.

■ **Place authority with key members.** Be clear about what authority different individuals have. Respect the various roles.

■ **Be positive about colleagues.** Take opportunities to affirm one another rather than being critical. Be as positive as possible.

■ **Recognize the individual.** Learn to listen and respect each individual as unique; recognize that they have a need deep inside them to express themselves as a distinct person.

"Teamwork is the ability to work together toward a common vision. The ability to direct individual accomplishments toward organizational objectives. It is the fuel that allows common people to attain uncommon results." **Andrew Carnegie**

■ **Discuss differences.** If a problem arises, try to distinguish details of the actual incident that took place; the emotions involved, and questions of identity that have been raised. Sometimes our assumptions about others' intentions are wrong. If you need to confront a member of the team, do it privately, not publicly. Present criticisms as suggestions or questions if you can.

■ **Build trust.** Try to foster a safe environment in which colleagues trust one another and can talk about their development needs.

■ **Value diversity.** Give credence to different opinions on minor matters.

■ **Don't apportion blame.** Blame is unproductive; instead identify the real issues and seek creative ways of resolving conflict. Equally, if you've been responsible for a task that has gone well, don't boast about it.

■ **Believe in the identity of the team.** Remember the acronym TEAM: Together Everyone Achieves More.

Make sure each person knows not only the team's overall goals but also their own individual responsibilities.

Mindpower **secrets**

7.3

Handle your boss better

One common cause of stress is dealing with a boss. Your boss may be hopeless at organizing things and constantly changing his or her mind about priorities. Their instructions may not be clear and they may raise their voice when they feel that their directions haven't been followed.

Alternatively, maybe your boss does give clear instructions, but hovers over you to make sure you are carrying out all their wishes. You, therefore, don't feel trusted to get on with the job. In either situation, you can end up feeling not valued and frustrated, which can lead to stress.

case study A friend, Barry, confided in me that he was having terrible trouble with his boss and was losing confidence in his own abilities. Barry has a sharp mind, so I was surprised by this. As Barry talked, he revealed that his boss, Greg, was under pressure and was constantly changing his mind about priorities and moving the goal posts. Barry felt as if he could no

Here are some tips on managing your boss:

■ **Consider your boss's style of working.** Get underneath their surface behaviour patterns and think about them as a person. A good boss will want to get the best out of their staff. Unfortunately, every boss has areas of insecurity and these will become clear over time.

■ **Schedule regular meetings with your boss.** This creates a chance to regularly review your work and how effectively you have done it. Make it clear that you want to learn.

■ **Clarify instructions.** Ask for clarification if you're unsure about instructions. There's no point writing a 20-page report if your boss only wants 5 pages. This is best done in face-to-face communication, rather than by email – if you ask these questions in an email, you may well go backwards and forwards without making real progress.

■ **Agree priorities.** Sit down with your boss and agree on the major priorities he or she wants you to follow. This is particularly crucial if your boss keeps adding to your workload. If so, you will need to agree the main purpose of your job and the priorities required to fulfil that purpose. When you have decided these, work out with your boss which of your activities fulfil these priorities and which do not. Then be ruthless: avoid activities that do not fulfil the agreed priorities.

Clarify instructions from your boss and seek agreement on your priorities.

longer successfully complete tasks and was failing. I suggested that, from then on, Barry should get written instructions from his boss or else write down his interpretation of them and get Greg to OK them. The latter case worked best: together they were able to clarify and amend instructions before work began and Barry was able to resume his usual high standard of work.

7.4

Assert yourself

If you say yes every time someone asks you to help them with a task, you will never learn to manage your work properly – you may even become stressed. Part of looking after yourself is remaining in control of the work you have to do. You therefore need to learn to assert yourself and say no at times.

Saying no is difficult: we tend to think that, if we say no, we might hurt people's feelings or spoil our chances in the future. But if we don't, we can become stressed and cannot complete tasks as well as we'd like. Here are some guidelines on how to assert yourself and say no:

■ **First, think about your own priorities and goals.** Does the task being suggested fit in with the priorities and goals your boss has set you (see Secret 7.3) or you have set yourself? If it does, then consider it; if it doesn't, reject it.

■ **Consider the knock-on effects.** Think about the effects of taking on more work. Would you have to delay completing other tasks? What would be the result for your wider life?

"Never allow a person to tell you no who doesn't have the power to say yes"

Eleanor Roosevelt, columnist and humanitarian

■ **Realize you have a right to say no.** You do not have to accept everything that comes your way.

■ **Be fair to yourself.** In taking care of your own wellbeing and in order to work effectively, you must be fair to yourself, as well as to others. You have a right to express your own point of view, just as much as the other person has.

■ **Assert yourself firmly.** Be positive. If you're turning something down, suggest other choices that could be followed up. Don't feel you have to apologize. Learn to be firm and direct – neither aggressive nor timid. Practise making such statements as: "I'd love to be involved that afternoon, but I've already got plans"; "It's nice to be asked, but I can't help you at the moment"; "I need to check my diary – ask me again later" (not "I'll come back to you later", which would put a burden on you). If your boss is asking you to take on another task, put the responsibility for the decision on him or her and say, "This is what I'm working on at the moment – which do you want me to do?"

Realize you have a right to say no. You do not have to accept everything that comes your way.

7.5

Make the most of your time

To look after yourself in business you need to keep your mind active. You need to work not only efficiently – making good use of resources and with systems in place so that things go smoothly – but also effectively, in order to make something of your life – to make it count and achieve something positive.

Here's my advice on ways that can help you to make the most of your working life:

■ **Maintain your life priorities.** Set certain priorities in your life, and stick to them. Develop plans that derive from your priorities.
■ **Plan your time well.** There's no substitute for scheduling if you want to maximize the use of your time and avoid wasting it.
■ **Divide and conquer work.** Separate large tasks into smaller, more manageable units. Work on one task at a time and do that to the best of your ability.
■ **Be organized.** Set up systems for routine tasks. Put things back in a certain place when you have finished with them.

■ **Exploit your most productive time.** Know what time of day you work best and do your best to protect that time in order to complete tasks that require the most thought.

■ **Use time effectively.** Work in concentrated periods but also make sure you take regular breaks. Deal with the urgent and important tasks as much as possible. Have less important tasks available to work on in your slack time.

■ **Delegate where you can.** When you're doing this, remember to always give clear instructions so that the operation is effective.

■ **Keep clear communication lines with your boss.** Clarify your role with your boss and the expectations he or she has of you.

■ **Use meetings efficiently.** Make better use of meetings and communicate by email and phone more effectively.

■ **Keep a lid on the stress levels.** Develop ways that work for you to reduce stress.

However small the task, doing it right first time is the best, most effective – and least stressful – use of time.

7.6

Keep an open mind

The final Secret in this book focuses not only on keeping your mind active and sharp but also on keeping it curious, receptive and interested in exploring new things. You should want to learn new skills, and actually put those good intentions into practice.

Here are some ways to help you keep developing as a person with an open mind:

■ **Don't settle for an ordinary life.** Be expectant, and try to live the life you want to live. Don't stay with the familiar. Imagine yourself in old age – do you want to feel you have really achieved something? Then start on that journey by taking the first step now.

case study A few years ago Rob felt he had achieved everything he had striven for he had a good job, a nice home and a growing family. He was dissatisfied, however. After years of trying to reach the top of the career ladder, he had arrived there, but still life didn't make sense. He had to re-evaluate his life, not just his business life, so he began to work with his family in a

■ **Seek new horizons.** Think of new challenges that can captivate you and stretch you.

■ **Don't fixate on difficulties.** You shouldn't get weighed down by fears and negative thinking about what you cannot do and what you are not good at. Rise above such thoughts. Ask friends and colleagues to help you identify your strengths.

■ **Use the power of your imagination.** Visualize yourself being successful in a new skill you have always wanted to learn. Then begin to go for it!

■ **Look for the positive.** Practise being positive when difficulties come. You may not be able to change the problems that come up, but you can change your response to them. Don't ignore difficulties; they won't go away, so face up to them.

■ **Keep looking forward.** As you grow older, the temptation is to become more taken up with the past. Resist that temptation: focus on what you can do today and tomorrow, next month and next year.

■ **Now is the moment.** Don't wait for the right time to come before you start something new. If you wait for such a time, you'll wait forever. Start something new now!

Think of a new challenge that can stretch you ... and take a step towards fulfilling that challenge today.

local community club that helped new workers and their families settle into his home city. Unsure at first, he and his family gradually got to know many new people and were able to help them; they themselves learnt a lot too about new cultures. By focusing on something outside his work, Rob grew as a whole person – which made his working life more effective as well.

Jargon buster

Acronym
A word formed from the initial letters of other words, e.g. STAIR for 'Scope, Target, Analysis, Interpretation and Recommendations'.

Alliteration
The use of the same letter at the beginning of words. It can be used to help as a memorable expression in a presentation.

Appreciative inquiry
A way of solving problems that focuses on valuing existing people and systems while exploring future possibilities.

Auditory learners
See learning styles.

Bar chart
A bar chart has bars of equal width but with different heights in proportion to the values they stand for. They are useful for comparing quantities over time.

Brainstorming
A meeting in which participants put forward as many ideas and suggestions as they can think of.

Closed question
A question that can be answered by a simple 'yes' or 'no'. See also open question.

Demographic
The characteristics of a population or community relating to the study of the changes (numbers of births, deaths, marriages, cases of disease, etc) occurring in it over time.

Disposable income
The amount of income you have left after you have paid income tax and social security charges, pension contributions, etc.

Flow chart
A flow chart illustrates a series of steps and is useful to show the stages of a process.

Gist-read
To read so as gain an overall idea of the text.

Infer
To understand a writer's or speaker's (often implicit) purpose in a text or talk.

Intensive reading
Gaining a lot of detailed understanding of information by closely reading a text.

Kinesthetic learners
See learning styles.

Learning styles

The different ways in which people learn. Visual learners like to see information in pictures, diagrams, charts, tables and in writing. Auditory learners like to listen to information and then discuss it with others, listening to all opinions to help them learn. Kinesthetic learners like to be active and learn by doing.

Line graph

A line graph shows the relationship between two kinds of information (along the vertical and horizontal axes) and how they vary, depending on each other. It is useful to show changes or trends over time.

Mnemonic

Something used as a way to help you remember something else.

Open question

A question that cannot be answered by a simple 'yes' or 'no' (see closed question), but means that the person giving the answer needs to think and develop their response. Open questions might begin with the words 'why' or 'how'.

Paraphrase

To express something using different words.

Pareto principle

A rule expressing the fact that approximately 80% of effects (e.g. business sales) come from 20% of causes (e.g. your main customers). Also called the 80/20 rule.

Pattern diagram

A creative diagram that you draw to generate and capture ideas around a central key word.

PEST analysis

An analysis of Political, Economic, Social and Technological (PEST) changes that may influence a business.

Scan-read

To read a text in order to find a specific piece of information.

Skim-read

To read very quickly so as to gain an overall idea of the text.

SWOT analysis

An analysis of a business's Strengths, Weaknesses, Opportunities and Threats (SWOT).

Thesaurus

A dictionary of synonyms, arranged either by theme (in the style of *Roget's Thesaurus*: see Further Reading) or alphabetically.

USP

The Unique Selling Point (USP) of a company's product or service.

Visual learners

See learning styles.

Further reading

Augsburger, David *Caring Enough to Hear and to Be Heard* (Regal Books, 1982) ISBN 978 083 0708369

Bechtle, Mike *Confident Conversation* (Revell, 2008) ISBN 978 0 8007 3242 4

Bigwood, Sally and Spore, Melissa *Presenting Numbers, Tables and Charts* (Oxford University Press, 2003) ISBN 978 019 8607229

de Bono, Edward *Serious Creativity: Using the Power of Lateral Thinking to Create New Ideas* (Harper Collins, 1995) ISBN 978 0 00 63 79 584

de Bono, Edward *Six Thinking Hats* (Penguin Books, 1990) ISBN 978 014 0137842

Buzan, Tony *Mind Mapping* (BBC, 2006) ISBN 978 0563 520344

Davidson, George *Roget's Thesaurus of English Words and Phrases* (Penguin Books, 2004) ISBN 978 0140515039

Hargie, Owen (Editor) *The Handbook of Communication Skills* (3rd edition, Routledge, 2006) ISBN 978 0 415 35911 5

Kourdi, Jeremy *Business Strategy: A Guide to Taking Your Business Forward* (The Economist/Profile Books, 2009) ISBN 978 184 668 124 0

Manser, Martin H. *1001 Words You Need to Know and Use: An A-Z of Effective Vocabulary* (Oxford University Press, 2010) ISBN 978 019 956005 9

Manser, Martin H. (Editor) *Chambers Thesaurus* (3rd edition, Chambers, 2009) ISBN 978 0550 103338

Websites

For courses by Martin Manser on Report writing and English Grammar: www.martinmanser.com/M/MMTraining.aspx

For courses led by Martin Manser on Confident Written Communication, Organizing Effective Meetings, Leadership, and Time Management (University of the Arts London: London College of Communication):

www.lcc.arts.ac.uk/shortcourses/confident_written_communications.htm

www.lcc.arts.ac.uk/shortcourses/effective_meetings.htm

www.lcc.arts.ac.uk/shortcourses/leadership_skills.htm

www.lcc.arts.ac.uk/shortcourses/time_management.htm

For courses on which Martin Manser is an Associate Trainer leading courses on writing (Capita Learning and Development):

www.capita-LD.co.uk

A website with visual mind-mapping software that enables users to interact visually with information:

www.mindjet.com

Guidance on developing skills in business (e.g. in memory, problem solving and decision making):

www.mindtools.com

Mindpower **secrets**

www.BusinessSecrets.net